COCO CHANEL

Pearls, Perfume, and the
Little Black Dress

Susan Goldman Rubin

ABRAMS BOOKS FOR YOUNG READERS

NEW YORK

Cataloging-in-Publication Data has been applied for and may be obtained
from the Library of Congress.

ISBN 978-1-4197-2544-9

Text copyright © 2018 Susan Goldman Rubin
Book design by Erich Lazar

Printed and bound in China
10 9 8 7 6 5 4 3 2 1

Abrams Books for Young Readers are available at special discounts when purchased in
quantity for premiums and promotions as well as fundraising or educational use.
Special editions can also be created to specification.
For details, contact specialsales@abramsbooks.com or the address below.

ABRAMS The Art of Books
195 Broadway, New York, NY 10007
abramsbooks.com

For Elaina Ann Rubin and
Olivia Juliet Rubin

CONTENTS

Coco wearing a knit jersey suit with a pocketed cardigan and her trademark strings of pearls, 1929

INTRODUCTION
Who Was Coco Chanel?

Her name stands for style. The little black dress. Strings of pearls tossed casually over a sweater. Quilted shoulder bags on chain straps. The perfume Chanel Nº 5.

> I make fashions women can live in, feel comfortable in.

"Chanel is France's greatest figure," wrote her friend the novelist Paul Morand. Yet he noted her temper and sarcasm as well as her brilliance. She was a controversial celebrity, an innovator with an eye for fashion and a talent for business that made her enormously successful. At the same time, many regarded Chanel as an opportunist, a tyrant, a chronic liar, and a snob. Some even suspected her of being a Nazi sympathizer during World War II. Still, women everywhere were in awe of the Chanel brand and the products that bore her distinctive label. Coco designed clothes that she wore herself, and she was her own best model. Her friend surrealist artist Salvador Dalí said,

All her life,
all she did was change
men's clothing
into women's.

The marketplace in Saumur, Maine-et-Loire, the town where Coco was born

SELL HER
TO THE
GYPSIES

○○○○○○○○○○○○○○○○○○○○○○○○○○○

Coco was born in a poorhouse, a place for homeless people, in the town of Saumur, France, on August 19, 1883. Later, she invented a different version of her beginnings, but biographers have pieced together the true account. Coco's childhood colored her whole life.

Since her father, a peddler, was on the road when she was born, two workers from the charity hospital went to the city hall to record her birth. Coco's mother was still too weak to attend. When the mayor asked for the baby's last name, no one knew how to spell it, so he incorrectly wrote "Chasnel." Chanel never changed her birth certificate for fear of revealing the truth about her poor family.

1

At her baptism, a day after she was born, she was named Gabrielle. Later Coco lied and said that the nun who'd held her also gave her the middle name "Bonheur," meaning "happiness," as a good-luck charm. Coco disliked the name Gabrielle because her mother hadn't chosen it, and she claimed that her father didn't like it either. She later told friends that he had called her "Little Coco," a nickname she really acquired as a young woman.

Her parents were not married, and therefore Coco and her older sister, Julia, were illegitimate, a mark of disgrace in those days. Their parents finally married in November 1884. The family traveled from town to town in south-central France in a horse-drawn buggy. At markets and fairs, Coco's father sold bonnets that he had bought from a hatter. Her mother helped him and sold things at her own stall. More babies quickly came along: a son, Alphonse, and another daughter, Antoinette. By the time Coco was six, her exhausted mother was suffering terribly from asthma. Her great-uncle Augustin invited the family to stay at his house in the country, but Coco's restless father did not stay long, instead wandering off to drink at taverns and chase the ladies. After a while Coco's mother went in search of him, leaving the children behind.

"No childhood was less gentle," said Coco. "All too soon I realized that life was a serious matter." One night she and her siblings were put to bed in their great-uncle's workroom. Bunches of grapes stored for the winter in paper bags hung from the rafters. Coco threw a pillow at a bag and it fell down. Delighted, she kept throwing pillows until she had burst all the bags and grapes covered the wooden floor. "For the first time in my life I was whipped," she recalled. "The humiliation was something I would never forget." One of her aunts predicted she would "turn out badly." Another said, "We'll have to sell her to the gypsies." At that time, Gypsies, or Roma, had come to France from Bohemia. They were wanderers, and Coco most likely saw them at the markets and fairs where her parents peddled their goods.

All too soon
I realized that life
was a serious
matter.

Coco at age nine spent hours playing by herself in the churchyard cemetery. "I was the queen of this secret garden," she remembered. She talked to the dead and sometimes brought rag dolls that she had made to decorate the tombstones.

Meanwhile, her mother caught up with her father, and they had two more babies: a son, Lucien, and then another

Nuns in prayer at the Aubazine convent-orphanage

boy, Augustin, who died in infancy. When Coco was ten, her mother left her other children with Great-Uncle Augustin and took Coco and Julia with her to join their father at an inn where he worked as a waiter. During the cold winter, Coco's frail mother came down with bronchitis and ran a high fever. She died on February 16, 1895. Coco was eleven.

None of their relatives wanted to take care of Coco and her siblings. Her brothers were placed at a farm to earn their keep. And Coco, Julia, and Antoinette went to an orphanage in Aubazine run by the sisters of the Congregation of the Sacred Heart of Mary.

I AM
NOT AN
ORPHAN!

ooooooooOOOOOOOOOOOOOooooooo

ater in life Coco never used the word "orphanage." Instead, she said her father took her to stay with unmarried "aunts" who always dressed in gray and black. "My aunts were good people, but absolutely without tenderness," she would say. "I was not loved in their house." She told the girls at the orphanage that her father had gone to America to seek his fortune and would come to get her as soon as he was rich. But in reality, after he dropped her off, Coco never saw him again.

Aubazine had been a monastery. The steep-roofed stone building stood on a plateau, surrounded by a forest. Inside, the walls were whitewashed, and the doors to the dormitories were painted black. Coco and the orphans wore white blouses and black skirts. The nuns had white wimples and black skirts.

The nuns' cleanliness and stark simplicity pleased Coco. Fresh linens piled in high cupboards and the smell of the yellow soap the girls used to scrub their faces left lasting impressions. The geometric loops in the stained glass windows suggested interlocking Cs.

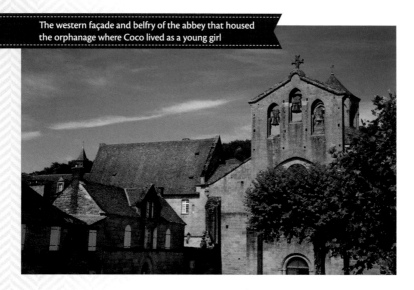

The western façade and belfry of the abbey that housed the orphanage where Coco lived as a young girl

The orphans followed a strict routine from early Mass to bedtime prayers. Six days a week they went to classes. In the evenings, they learned to sew simple things such as hems on sheets for their trousseaux, collections of household linens assembled for when they married. Every Sunday they hiked through the woods after church. Coco detested the regimen: Prayers. Silence. Prayers. She hated to kneel in the abbey,

6

and she made up stories to tell the priest in confession. She pretended that she didn't understand a word of the catechism, but she did. Coco learned and remembered the nuns' lessons about how the Jews had crucified Jesus. At that time, the beginning of the twentieth century, Catholic institutions such as Aubazine instructed children to hate Jews. A friend later wrote, "Chanel's anti-Semitism was not only verbal; but passionate . . . and often embarrassing."

Coco stayed at Aubazine for almost seven years. During holidays, she and her sisters visited their paternal grandparents in Moulins and their aunts Louise and Adrienne in Varennes. Louise, the oldest of nineteen children, was married to a railroad stationmaster. Aunt Adrienne was just a year older than Coco. Coco adored her. They looked like sisters and pretended they were. At night they shared an attic bedroom in Varennes and talked till dawn. As teenagers, they secretly read romance novels that were published in installments in the paper. "We cut out the serial from the newspaper and sewed them all together," remembered Coco.

The stories, such as *Two Little Vagrants*, told of poor girls who became rich, elegant ladies. "Those novels taught me about life," Coco said. "They nourished my sensibility and my pride." She smuggled the romances back to Aubazine, where pulp fiction was absolutely forbidden, and hid them in the attic. Once, she slipped pages into her notebook and copied excerpts during a creative-writing test. After her teacher read her essay, she made Coco confess about her private library and took the romances away.

Coco longed for beautiful clothes and was captivated by a description of a heroine's lavender dress with ruffles. While visiting her aunts, she asked for permission to have the local seamstress make a dress for her. Unbeknownst to her aunts, Coco gave the seamstress detailed instructions for whipping up a dress like the one in the novel. "It had a high neck with flying ribbons and matching slip, purple, and underneath a ruffle," recalled Coco. "I was perhaps fifteen or sixteen."

On a Sunday morning Coco put on the formfitting dress and came downstairs to go to Mass. Her aunt Louise took one look at her and ordered her to go upstairs and change into proper clothing. Girls of her age were to wear modest tailored suits without ribbons, ruffles, or saucy purple slips. Despite Coco's tears, the lavender creation went back to the dressmaker. But the allure of ruffles stayed with Coco.

Aunt Louise was a skilled seamstress, too, and she taught Coco and Adrienne how to stitch beautiful tablecloths, start a pleat by breaking the cloth with a thumb, and make a complicated sleeve. When Louise bought new hats in the resort town of Vichy, she showed them off to Coco and Adrienne. Armed with scissors, she reshaped the brims and trimmed the hats with streamers and braid. The girls helped her transform ordinary bonnets into marvels. Coco was impressed and inspired.

In 1901, Coco turned eighteen. She and her sister Julia were too old to stay at Aubazine, unless they wanted to become nuns. So their grandmother enrolled them at Notre-Dame, a finishing school for young ladies in Moulins. It was a time when the French were hotly debating what was known as the Dreyfus Affair, which involved the arrest and wrongful conviction for treason of Captain Alfred Dreyfus, a French officer of Alsatian Jewish descent. The scandal stirred up anti-Semitism in the Catholic community in Moulins, including in Coco.

View of Place d'Allier, Moulins, the town where Coco and her aunt Adrienne went to Notre-Dame finishing school and then worked as seamstresses

Her younger sister, Antoinette, remained at Aubazine. Coco and Julia were charity cases at Notre-Dame and earned their keep by doing such chores as peeling vegetables, scrubbing floors, and making beds. They wore special black outfits to distinguish them from the others. All the girls were strictly chaperoned, and their outings consisted of going to Mass on Sundays. Occasionally Coco was allowed to take the train to Vichy to visit her sick grandfather at the spa there. "Vichy was a fairyland," she said. The elegant hotels, gardens, and orchestra playing in the bandstand enchanted her. "I watched the eccentric people parade past," she recalled, "and I said to myself, 'I would become one of them.'"

WHO HAS
SEEN COCO?

By the time Coco was twenty, she had left Notre-Dame and gone to work with her aunt Adrienne at a lingerie shop in Moulins. At first the young women shared an attic bedroom above the store. Soon after they arrived, however, Coco moved to a cheap room in town. During the week Coco continued in her job at the lingerie shop, and on Sundays she and Adrienne worked in a tailor's shop. Officers came in to have their uniforms mended and altered, and they flirted with the young women. Although Coco was too short and thin to be considered beautiful by the day's standards, she charmed the men.

One afternoon some lieutenants invited Coco and Adrienne to go out for sherbet. Another time the soldiers took them to a café concert at La Rotonde. During intermissions, amateur girls stood up to sing and keep the audience entertained. The officers dared Coco to sing. She leaped onstage and sang a popular song about a Parisian young lady who has lost her dog at the amusement park.

"I've lost my poor Coco. Coco, my lovable dog. Who has seen Coco?"

The audience loved it and shouted, "Coco! Coco!" demanding an encore. From then on, she was dubbed "*la petite Coco*"—"little Coco."

One of her admirers was Étienne Balsan, a young cavalry officer from the Tenth Light Horse Brigade, a regiment of aristocratic gentlemen. Étienne asked Coco out and became her boyfriend.

Around that time, she decided to leave Moulins and move to Vichy to pursue her dream of becoming a singer. "You won't get anywhere," said Étienne. "You don't have a voice, and you sing like a trombone."

Nevertheless, he helped her. Adrienne had agreed to go with Coco, and Étienne paid for material that the young women used to make new dresses and hats. After they arrived in Vichy, they posed for a photograph sporting their homemade outfits. Coco took singing lessons and rented a sparkly black sequined gown for auditions at the casino and theaters. No one hired her. The gown was returned, but she never forgot its glamour.

Adrienne finally went back to Moulins. Meanwhile, Étienne visited Coco in Vichy. He was now out of the army and had bought a country estate called Royallieu with a small château, stables, and paddocks. Coco said, "How lucky you are to have racehorses!" Étienne invited her to come see the horses train. She did and wound up staying at Royallieu. According to Coco, she was only sixteen at the time, "too young to be away from home." But she really was twenty-one and had no home. She invented stories about her background for Étienne and said she had run away. "I had told him lies about my miserable childhood," she later admitted. Coco did not expect Étienne to propose marriage, since she was a seamstress without a dowry. She knew he would marry a society woman of his own class. So Coco just enjoyed life as a guest at the luxurious château.

At Royallieu she learned to ride horses and spent days galloping through the forests. A local tailor made her jodhpurs, snug riding pants, from a stable boy's pattern even though most women at that time wore long skirts and rode sidesaddle. If a woman dared to wear trousers on a Paris street in those days, she risked being arrested. Coco liked dressing in men's riding trousers, and not just when she was riding. She also decked herself out in mannish high collars, knitted ties, and a soft felt hat worn over her pigtail.

A friend visiting the estate described her: "She was a tiny little thing, with a pretty, very expressive, roguish face and a strong personality. She amazed us because of her nerve on horseback."

Étienne took her to the fashionable Longchamp Race-course in the Bois de Boulogne in Paris. Society ladies wore elaborate dresses and huge feathered hats to the races. Coco, however, appeared in a schoolgirl's suit and a straw boater and caused a sensation! Inspired by her aunt Louise, she had bought the hat at a department store and trimmed it herself. "Whoever makes your hats?" asked women. An idea began taking shape.

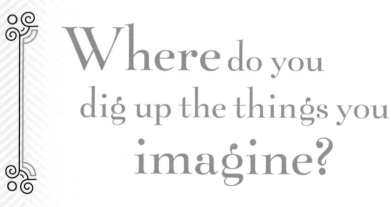

Where do you dig up the things you imagine?

After several years at Royallieu, Coco realized that she didn't want to spend the rest of her life depending on men. One day she said to Étienne, "I can't earn my living riding horses. I think I'd like to work." She told him her idea for making hats and opening a millinery shop. So he offered to let her use his apartment on Boulevard Malesherbes in Paris.

Around that time, he invited Coco to go to a foxhunt at a château in Pau, near the Pyrenees mountains. There, she

Coco's straw boater, 1954, a design she borrowed from the uniforms of sailors and schoolboys at the start of her career

met an English polo player, Arthur Capel, nicknamed "Boy," and fell deeply in love. Coco was twenty-seven, although she claimed to be eighteen. When Boy returned to Paris, she went with him, leaving Étienne a note: "Forgive me, but I love him."

In Boy's company she met sophisticated Parisians from high society. To keep up with their conversations, she made up stories. "I lied all the time," she said, "because I didn't want to be taken for a country bumpkin." Boy questioned her about it, but she explained that she was "just rearranging truth a bit."

"He really understood me," she recalled. "He said to me, 'Coco, if only you'd stop lying! Can't you talk like everyone else? Where do you dig up the things you imagine?'" Yet Boy appreciated her desire to work and respected her ambition. He agreed to finance Coco's hat shop in Étienne's ground-floor apartment. Both men wanted to help her.

Coco bought more flat-topped straw hats and boaters at the Galeries Lafayette department store and added a ribbon, a feather, or a flower or simply turned up a brim on one side. Étienne's friends flocked to her shop out of curiosity and brought *their* friends. Once, a woman came in, and when Coco asked if she could help her, the woman said, "I just came to have a look at *you*."

So Coco hired an assistant and stayed in the back room. When she was told a customer had asked to see her, she sent the assistant back out. "The more people came to call on me, the more I hid away," she recalled years later. "This habit has always remained with me. I never appeared at shows. One had to make conversation, which terrified me. And I didn't know how to sell."

Soon she needed more room and asked Étienne, who was still her friend, to support a move. He refused. But Boy believed in her ability. And he wanted her to have something to do while he was busy taking care of his family's shipping companies. "Coco is intelligent," he told an acquaintance, a society lady. "She has the qualities of a businesswoman." So

Galeries Lafayette, the busy department store in Paris, during a sale in the early 1900s

in 1911 he advanced Coco the money for renting commercial space at 21, rue Cambon—the start of the House of Chanel.

Sales increased so fast, Coco needed more assistants. She lured experienced fitters and salespeople away from prestigious fashion houses.

At the time, the leading fashion designer in Paris was Charles Frederick Worth, considered the father of high

French fashion, or haute couture. Worth had died in 1895, and his sons had taken over the business. Worth's luxurious dresses with bustles and trains were worn over tight boned corsets. Corsets were meant to shape a woman's body and were very uncomfortable. His rival, Jacques Doucet, created ornate evening gowns made of velvet and lace, also worn over armor-like corsets. Paul Poiret had trained with both Worth and Doucet and then opened his own fashion house. Poiret introduced loose, straight dresses and harem pants (pantaloons) inspired by the cultures of Turkey and Japan. He boasted that he had freed women from corsets. Coco sneered, "Paul Poiret, a most inventive couturier, dressed women in costumes." And he later said of her, "We ought to have been on guard against that boyish head. It was going to give us every kind of shock."

I WAS
MY OWN
MASTER

○○○○○○○○○○○○○○○○○○○○○○○○○○○○○

Inspired by her romance with Boy, Coco began decking herself out in his clothes. She borrowed things from his closet: polo shirts, loose sweaters, and English schoolboy–style blazers. Coco had already started wearing jodhpurs at Royallieu for horseback riding, but now Boy sent her to a tailor to have a riding jacket and trousers made out of the finest material.

Once, she and Boy attended a costume party at Royallieu where the guests dressed up for a mock country wedding. Coco was supposed to be the "best man." She bought trousers, a white shirt, a dark jacket, and ankle boots from the boys' department at a Paris department store. Although the outfit was meant for fun, Coco added a feminine touch with her alluring looks and charm. The tomboy clothes suited her and showed off her slim figure. While other women wore fussy feathers and lace, Coco purposely created an image of herself as a gamine, a playfully mischievous girl, and sparked a trend.

Her adoring patrons at rue Cambon urged her to expand her line and offer more than hats. So she began selling women turtleneck sweaters and open-neck polo shirts like the kind she took from Boy's closet.

Coco (on the right) and her aunt Adrienne outside Coco's Deauville boutique beneath the awning with her name, 1913

By 1913 Boy had encouraged Coco to open a branch of her shop in the seaside resort of Deauville, where they spent summers. They chose a spot on rue Gontaut-Biron, across the street from the Grand Casino. Coco hung out her first awning. Black letters against a striped background spelled out "Gabrielle Chanel." An article about Coco's "trendy new boutique" appeared in a women's magazine. The article included a photograph showing Coco in a long skirt, a simple blouse, and an oversize knit tunic with big patch pockets. In those days, pockets on the outside of clothes were part of a man's wardrobe and considered unladylike, but Coco liked sagging pockets and defied convention. She also pinned a camellia on her jacket the way men did, starting another signature style.

One day, the weather turned cold. Coco needed something warm to wear and took one of Boy's jersey sweaters. But she didn't want to pull it over her head, so she cut it down the front, finished the edge with ribbon, and added a collar and a knot. When she went out, people asked her, "Where did you find that dress?" Coco said, "If you like it, I'll sell it to you." Quickly she made and sold ten jersey dresses. Later she said, "My fortune is built on that old jersey I'd put on because it was cold in Deauville."

On the beach, she posed for photographs to promote her sporty clothes. "Everybody wanted to meet me," she recalled. "I became something of a celebrity, and there, too, I started a fashion—couturiers as stars."

The following summer, when Coco was again in Deauville, Germany declared war on France, and the next day Great Britain declared war on Germany. August 3, 1914, was the start of the Great War (World War I). Boy enlisted and joined a British intelligence unit.

By the third week of August, German troops had advanced toward Paris, and wealthy people fled to Deauville. Coco's was the only store open in town. Women needed practical outfits to do volunteer work in hospitals, and they snapped up Coco's skirts, sailor blouses, and knit jackets.

I created a brand-new silhouette.

Boy visited Coco whenever possible. In the summer of 1915, they went to a fashionable resort south of Biarritz, near the Spanish border. Spain was neutral, and the rich flocked there to escape from thoughts of war. Coco and Boy hit on the idea of opening a branch of her boutique in Biarritz. Once again they chose a key location: an ornate villa on rue Gardères, facing the casino near the beach. On July 15, 1915, Coco opened her shop, the first fashion house in Biarritz. She hired Marie-Louise Deray, an expert seamstress, and sent for her sister Antoinette. Before long she had sixty women sewing for her in Paris while also maintaining salons in Biarritz and Deauville.

Since there was a wartime shortage of fabric, Coco thought of making dresses out of inexpensive machine-knit wool jersey, the kind used for men's underwear and nightshirts. "The jersey in those days was only worn underneath," she said. "I gave it the honor of being worn on top."

She bought a manufacturer's entire stock, which came only in beige and gray, and transformed the fabric into chemise dresses. Coco shortened hems to above the ankle so that women could move freely. "I created a brand-new silhouette," she said. The dresses sold out! So she bought more jersey and had it dyed in a range of colors. Coco shaped the soft jersey right on the models, who had to stand still for hours. An assistant held pins while Coco barked commands.

"Mademoiselle was demanding," recalled Marie-Louise, the head of the workroom. "If a fitting went wrong [Coco] exploded. She loved to pester people . . . She was tough, unrelenting with the staff. But what she came up with was sensational, both chic and exceedingly simple."

In America, *Harper's Bazaar* published a picture of Coco's creation with the caption, "Chanel's charming chemise dress." The stretchy material clung to the figure, so the dresses had to be worn without corsets. Poiret had killed corsets, but his

clothes featured dizzying pleats and feathers. Coco's dresses were simple and sporty. She later said, "By inventing the jersey I liberated the body; I discarded the waist." Of course, women had to be "slim like Coco" to look good in the dresses.

> Our workrooms were like a fairyland, a veritable rainbow.

Orders flooded the Biarritz boutique. Customers included members of the Spanish royal family. By early 1916, while the war raged on, Coco employed three hundred people in her boutiques and traveled in a chauffeured Rolls-Royce.

She sent Marie-Louise back to Paris to take charge of the atelier (workroom) there. Soon Coco had five workrooms, including the headquarters in Paris, producing dresses in silk, cotton, and wool as well as jersey. She selected the fabrics and colors herself. "Our workrooms were like a fairyland, a veritable rainbow," recalled Marie-Louise.

Coco boasted that she had started another trend in 1917 by cutting her hair short. At that time, it was fashionable for women to have long hair. Coco's thick hair fell below her waist,

Coco with short hair, circa 1923

and when she went out in the evening she did it up in three braids wrapped around her head. One night she was dressing to go to the opera, and the gas burner in her bathroom blew up. Soot covered her white dress and her face, and her hair was singed. She washed her face, determined to go out.

"I took a pair of scissors and cut one braid off," she said. Then she cut the second braid and finally told her maid to cut the third. Coco slipped into a black dress and left for the opera. Everyone admired her coiffure, saying that she looked like "a young boy, a little shepherd." From then on, when planning a new collection, as a ritual she cut her models' hair and her own with a pair of nail scissors. But it was Poiret who had introduced short "bobbed" hair for women when he presented his 1908 collection. The clothes, inspired by ancient Greek gowns and Japanese kimonos, featured straight, geometric lines. Poiret wanted his models to have very spare hairdos to complement the outfits. So they wore Dutch-boy cuts with full bangs.

Coco must have known about her rival's innovation. Nevertheless, she gave another account of how *she* popularized the fad. "In 1917 I slashed my thick hair," she recalled. "To begin with I trimmed it bit by bit. Finally I wore it short. . . . And everyone went into raptures."

Coco's earnings enabled her to pay back the money Boy had loaned her to open the boutique in Biarritz. "I was my own master," she said, "and I depended on myself alone."

Heart-shaped earrings made of gold metal, red and black plastic, and rhinestones, 1995, that feature the double Cs linking the names Chanel and Capel

Yet she had always hoped that one day they would marry, despite her lower-class background. But in the spring of 1918, Boy became engaged to an English aristocrat, Diana Lister Wyndham. They married in October, just before the war ended. Coco was heartbroken.

She and Boy still cared about each other. Coco rented a villa in the town of Garches, west of Paris, and he visited her there. After seeing her in December 1919, he left in his chauffeured Rolls-Royce to meet his sister in Cannes. On the way there, a tire exploded. The Rolls flipped over and burst into flames. The driver escaped. Boy was killed on the spot. An old friend of Coco's drove to her villa that night to tell her about the accident, but she guessed what had happened and asked him to take her to Cannes. They drove for eighteen hours without stopping. No one saw her cry. "His death was a terrible blow to me," she later said. "1919, the year I woke up famous and the year I lost everything."

Coco's black wool jersey and silk satin day dress with pleated skirt, 1926

BLACK WIPES OUT EVERYTHING

C oco still had her three boutiques and plunged into work as a memorial to Boy. In his will, much of his estate went to his wife and baby daughter, but he had left Coco a huge sum of money, which she used to move to a five-story building at 31, rue Cambon. Later, in about 1928, she installed mirrors that covered every wall in the salon. Mirrors lined the walls of the staircase too. The faceted mirrors reflected multiple images of the models as they presented new collections. Coco, perched out of sight at the top of the stairs, could see the reactions of the spectators below.

Boy had introduced Coco to a circle of artistic friends that included a legendary model named Misia Sert. As a young woman Misia had posed for artists Pierre-Auguste Renoir, Henri de Toulouse-Lautrec, and Édouard Vuillard. Portraits of her appeared in posters, photographs, and paintings all over Paris. The first time she and Coco met, Misia admired Coco's fur-trimmed red velvet coat, and at the end of the evening Coco offered to give it to her.

Jean Cocteau and the cast of the ballet *Le Train Bleu* wearing Coco's costumes, 1922: (left to right) Lydia Sokolova, Anton Dolin, Jean Cocteau, Leon Woizikovsky, and Bronislava Nijinska

"Obviously I could not accept it," recalled Misia. "But her gesture had been so pretty that I found her completely bewitching." The next day Misia hurried over to rue Cambon, and the women became best friends. Sometimes they dressed in twin Chanel outfits.

After Boy's death, Misia sympathized with Coco. "I tried desperately to think of ways to distract her," she said. At Misia's dinner parties Coco met artists Pablo Picasso and Jean Cocteau, composer Igor Stravinsky, and Sergei Diaghilev, the director of Ballets Russes. The artists and writers didn't ask or care about her background; they simply admired her talent and wit. Coco did not need to fabricate stories for them—a vice she still indulged in among certain people.

A few years later, she created costumes for Cocteau's ballet *Le Train Bleu*, about rich vacationers traveling to Deauville, and Picasso designed the stage curtain and program. The costumes for men and women were based on Coco's own lines of sports clothes: swimsuits, tennis outfits with headbands, and striped sweaters. When Cocteau was asked why he had chosen Coco, he said, "Because she is the greatest couturiere of our age."

One evening at the Paris Opera House, Coco sat in her box seat and surveyed the gowns of the women in the audience. "All those gaudy . . . colors shocked me," she said. "Those reds, those greens, those electric blues . . . brought back into fashion by Paul Poiret, made me feel ill. . . . I remember only too well saying to someone sitting beside me: 'These colors are impossible. These women, I'm bloody well going to dress them in black.'"

Up till then, women had worn black only if they were in mourning. But in 1920 Coco made the color fashionable by introducing "the little black dress."

"I imposed black," she said, "for black wipes out everything else around." Using materials such as crepe and wool, she designed simple sheaths with rounded necklines, close-fitting sleeves, and skirts that fell just below the knee.

These women, I'm bloody well going to dress them in black.

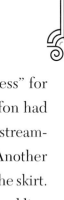

Coco made many versions of the "little black dress" for daytime and evening. One dress in sheer silk chiffon had floating panels and a pointed handkerchief hem with streamers at the shoulders that could be tied into bows. Another evening dress was sleeveless, with tiers of chiffon in the skirt. A severe, long-sleeved black dress featured a cowl neckline and resembled a nun's habit, a reflection of her days at the orphanage. Sometimes Coco added a white fabric camellia for contrast, and the flower became her symbol.

By 1926 the fame of Coco's creation had spread to America, and *Vogue* dubbed it the "Ford dress," comparing it to the mass-produced car that came only in black. Wealthy women on both sides of the Atlantic wore her designs or copies of them. Coco once said, "You have a style when everyone on the street is dressed like you. I achieved this."

The original Nº 5 perfume bottle designed in 1921, with a stopper marked with the double C logo

LEAD
THEM BY
THE NOSE

ºoooooooooOOOOOOOOoooooooooo

Each day, Coco came to work smelling of lye soap, the kind she had used at the orphanage. She loved perfume, however, and dabbed a drop behind her ears and at her wrists. In 1920 she began developing her own brand. "Women wear the perfumes they're given as presents," she once said. "You ought to wear your own, the one you like."

Other couturiers, such as Poiret, had established perfume and cosmetics businesses, but Coco was the first *not* to use floral scents. "I don't want hints of roses, of lilies of the valley," she told chemist Ernest Beaux, who had a laboratory in Grasse. "I want a perfume that is composed." Beaux experimented with aldehydes, new chemical compounds. Coco visited his lab every day and sniffed the specimens. Beaux presented two series: one through five, and twenty through twenty-four. Finally Coco chose number five. Five was her lucky number.

Since childhood Coco had been superstitious and thought that numbers were magical. The story goes that a gypsy once told her that five would bring her luck. Coco believed it "with a passion." She insisted that she had been born on August 5, although the true date was the nineteenth. However, her birth sign, Leo, was the fifth in the zodiac. And she always presented her fall dress collections on May 5, the fifth month of the year, and her spring collection on February 5.

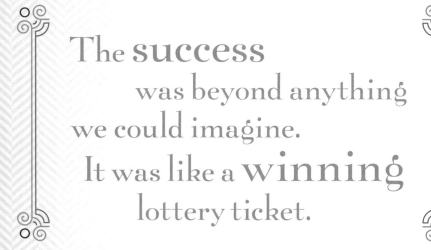

The success was beyond anything we could imagine. It was like a winning lottery ticket.

"That's what I expected," she said to Beaux of the fragrance she had selected. "A perfume unlike any other ever made."

She picked up the plain bottle, wrote "5" in her own hand, and said, "Now I will sell this."

That night she took a vial of the perfume to a swanky restaurant and sprayed women who passed her table. "You've got to be able to lead them by the nose," she said. Back in her Paris salon, she gave sample bottles to her favorite clients and had her salesgirls spray the fitting rooms with the scent. When her clients asked for more of the perfume, Chanel pretended that the idea of selling it had never occurred to her. "You mean you really like *my* perfume?" she asked coyly.

Beaux started producing Chanel Nº 5 while Coco explored packaging. At that time, most perfumes had romantic names such as *Mille et Une Nuits* (A Thousand and One Nights) and came packaged in containers etched with flowers or shaped like cupids. Coco preferred a plain, clear bottle revealing the "gold liquid within." Her friend Misia Sert said, "We experimented with a very severe bottle, ultra-simple, almost pharmaceutical, but in the Chanel style and with the elegant touch she gave to everything." A few weeks later the perfume reached selected stores. "The success was beyond anything we could have imagined," recalled Misia. "It was like a winning lottery ticket."

Coco asked Théophile Bader, co-owner of the department store Galeries Lafayette, to carry her perfume. He agreed but said his store and others would need a greater quantity than Beaux could produce in his lab. So he introduced her to his friends Pierre and Paul Wertheimer. The brothers had the largest perfume and cosmetics company in France and a network for distribution. The wealthy Wertheimers, who were Jewish, owned racehorses and arranged to have their first meeting with Coco at the elegant Longchamp Racecourse. Despite her anti-Semitism, Coco quickly came to a business agreement with them. The Wertheimers formed a partnership

Paul Wertheimer leading his winning colt, Lanvin, with jockey Rae Johnstone after victory in the English Derby at Epsom Downs, 1956

with Coco that lasted till the end of all their lives, but she and the brothers fought constantly.

Coco signed away her interests, or ownership, in the perfume business, keeping 10 percent of the profits instead, because she wanted to focus on her fashions. Later she regretted the split and said, "I let myself be swindled." She called Pierre "that bandit." He called her that "bloody woman" and hired a lawyer just to deal with her. But she made a fortune. Chanel N⁰ 5 is still a worldwide bestseller.

Coco launched the perfume on the fifth of May in 1921, when she presented her fall dress collection. From then on, an assistant at rue Cambon sprayed Chanel N⁰ 5 in the entrance to the building a moment before Coco arrived. And in her luxurious private apartment, Coco scattered the perfume on the curtains and the hot coals in her fireplace.

The Wertheimers also started producing Chanel lipstick. Coco always wore an intense shade of bloodred on her lips and had made the first stick herself in a tube of waxed paper. Then she designed a push-up case in gray that was stamped with a single *C*, her first logo. In 1925 she redid her logo with interlocking *C*s, which were not only her initials but also those of the union of Boy's last name and hers: Capel and Chanel. The double *C* also recalled the loops in the windows at Aubazine.

GO AND FETCH MY PEARLS

○○○○○○○○○○○○○○○○○○○○○○○○○○○○

A round this time, Coco dated Grand Duke Dmitri Pavlovich, a first cousin of the Russian tsar, Nicholas II. Dmitri had been involved in the murder of Grigori Rasputin, a charlatan who had befriended the Romanov imperial family. The Russian people had believed that Rasputin was ruling the country behind the scenes, and they had welcomed his death. But Tsar Nicholas punished Dmitri by ordering him to join the Russian Army at the Persian front. The Russian Empire and the British Empire were fighting the Ottoman Empire after their invasion of Persia (now Iran). Meanwhile, angry mobs rioted in Moscow, and in 1917 the Bolshevik Revolution began. The aristocracy of Russia fled for their lives.

Dmitri managed to make his way to London, then France. He had little money, but he had taken precious heirloom jewels with him, and he gave Coco ropes of pearls and gold chain necklaces. Pearls complemented her tanned skin and dark eyes and set off a simple black dress or a suit. In her opinion a suit was "naked" without jewelry. "Go and fetch my pearls," she ordered a maid once. "I will not go up to the ateliers until I have them around my neck."

Expensive jewelry does not improve the woman who wears it. If she looks plain, she will remain so.

Dmitri's gifts inspired her to start designing and selling costume jewelry, and she wore masses of fake pearls with the real thing. "I couldn't wear my own real pearls without being stared at on the street," she said, "so I started the vogue of wearing false ones." Coco believed that jewelry should be worn as an ornament and not to flaunt wealth. "Expensive jewelry does not improve the woman who wears it," she said. "If she looks plain, she will remain so."

Coco wearing strands of fake pearls and costume jewelry bracelets, 1936

Through Dmitri, the composer Igor Stravinsky, and Sergei Diaghilev's Ballets Russes, Coco discovered Russian folk art, which influenced her fashion designs. In the early 1920s she entered what she termed her "Slav period," using colorful Russian embroidery on plain black or neutral material. Dmitri also introduced her to his sister, Grand Duchess Marie Pavlovna.

After fleeing Russia, Marie had reunited with Dmitri. As a child, she had learned to sew, knit, and embroider. Exiled first in London and then in Paris, she needed a means of supporting herself, and made dresses. In 1921 she met Coco, hoping to get some useful suggestions for succeeding in the dressmaking business. "This unusual woman crossed my path at precisely the right time," recalled Marie.

During a visit to Coco's private studio on rue Cambon, Marie witnessed an argument between Coco and Madame Bataille, the woman who did embroidery for the House of Chanel. They were examining a crimson silk blouse that Madame Bataille had just finished based on a design Coco had found on Scottish sweaters. Coco refused to pay the high price Madame Bataille demanded, and Marie impulsively offered to do the job for less money. But the embroidery had to be done on a machine to produce the quantity Coco needed. So Marie quickly bought the simplest kind of embroidery sewing machine and learned how to use it. Three months later she delivered an embroidered blouse to Coco for the lower price. Coco bought the blouse and ordered many more.

Marie was thrilled. She hired three young Russian women to help her fill the orders and established a workshop that she named Kitmir, after a friend's Pekinese lapdog.

In the beginning of January 1922 Coco was preparing her spring collection, to be shown on February 5. Coco didn't sketch her designs. Instead, she worked with scissors hanging from a long white ribbon around her neck and cut, pinned, and shaped the muslin test garments (toiles) directly on the models.

Marie said, "I watched Chanel's creative genius express itself through her fingers . . . I can still see her sitting on her taboret . . . She would be dressed in a dark skirt and a sweater. The models would be called in one by one . . . A girl would walk into the room and up to Mlle. Chanel, who sat with a pair of scissors in her hand. This was the only moment when Chanel would look up at the model's face. Then the fitting began. The fitter standing beside her handed her the pins."

Pushing and pulling the fabric, Coco often pricked a model with the pins. If the model yowled in pain, Coco laughed. "Stand straight, girl," she would hiss through the pins in her mouth.

"No one spoke except Chanel," wrote Marie. "Sometimes she would be giving instructions or explaining some detail.

An embroidered silk crepe dress in the Slavic style for Chanel's spring/summer collection, 1921

Sometimes she would criticize and undo the work already done. Chanel, intent on her work . . . talked on without taking notice of anybody."

Back at Kitmir, Marie and her workers turned out blouses, tunics, and shift dresses in a Slavic style. One dress featured exquisite red and green embroidery bordering the short sleeves, V-neck, dropped waist, and shoulders. The back of the dress had rows of tiny green and red stitches running from the shoulders to the waist. The label read "Gabrielle Chanel," written in yellow script on black cloth, with the word "PARIS" in capital letters. This was the way Coco marked her clothing at that time.

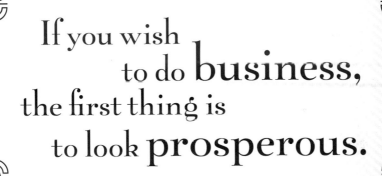

If you wish to do **business,** the first thing is to look **prosperous.**

On February 5, Marie hurried to rue Cambon for the showing and sat at the top of the mirrored staircase with Coco. At three o'clock the models "began to parade," wrote Marie. "When the first dress appeared which had my embroidery on it I almost cried out loud." By six o'clock the show had ended, and buyers were excitedly demanding the embroidered pieces.

The style became so popular that Coco introduced a version of the *roubachka*, the long, belted blouse worn by Russian peasant women. Magazines dubbed it "The Peasant Look." Marie hired more workers and soon had fifty employees.

But Coco later claimed that *she* had set up the embroidery workshop and put Marie in charge. It pleased Coco, a descendant of peasants, to employ titled royalty such as the Grand Duchess Marie.

After Coco and Marie had presented their first showings of embroidered clothing, Coco criticized Marie's dowdy appearance. "It is a great mistake for you to go round looking like a refugee," said Coco. "If you wish to do business, the first thing is to look prosperous." Coco taught Marie how to use makeup and said that her old-fashioned hairstyle resembled "a giant brioche on the top of her head." Taking a pair of scissors, Coco hacked off Marie's hair and gave her a short bob like her own. "When she had finished," reminisced Marie, "we were equally dismayed at the result. But the damage was done, and ever since that day, my hair has been short. It took many weeks, however, before my hairdresser could make my head look to some degree presentable."

However, Marie felt grateful to Coco for her advice and business and continued producing embroideries for her.

After Coco presented couture pieces for a new collection, dressmakers and manufacturers would turn out knockoff versions at lower prices. Buyers from department stores purchased originals and had them copied and produced in large numbers. "Come to my place and steal all the ideas you

Coco borrowed the Duke of Westminster's coat on a chilly night at the Chester horse races, 1924.

Coco Chanel wearing her "sailor" outfit

can," Coco told the press. She knew that the cheaper imitations could never be mistaken for her superb tailoring and fine fabrics meant for rich clients, celebrities, and royalty.

In 1924 she became interested in British and Scottish tweeds when she began a romance with Hugh Richard Arthur Grosvenor, the Second Duke of Westminster. The duke, nicknamed Bendor, was the richest man in Great Britain, but he liked to wear old jackets and faded golf sweaters. Coco dipped into his wardrobe and borrowed his tweed blazers, and then created feminine versions. Bendor bought a textile mill for her so she could manufacture her own wools for suits and coats.

In 1925 she introduced the prototype of what was to become the classic Chanel suit, with a collarless cardigan jacket, braided trim, patch pockets, and an A-line skirt. Bendor's yacht, *The Flying Cloud*, gave her another idea. She designed flared pants like the ankle-length bell-bottoms worn by the crew, because she said it was the only way to comfortably climb on and off a boat. The style caught on and started a universal trend of women wearing trousers. Coco even designed a beret like the yachting caps Bendor gave to his guests, and she wore hers with a jeweled pin.

Bendor lavished magnificent jewels upon her: rubies, diamonds, emeralds, and more pearls. "It is disgusting to wander around loaded down with millions around the neck just because one happens to be rich," she said. Coco kept most of the jewels locked up in a vault. Bendor's gifts, however, inspired her to open costume jewelry workshops that produced imitations of the elaborate necklaces and cuffs.

Coco joined Bendor at his estate, Eaton Hall, or at one of his country houses whenever she could, and they went hunting and fishing. In 1927 at Bendor's château in Mimizan, France, she met his friend Winston Churchill, the future prime minister. Churchill wrote to his wife, Clementine, "The famous Coco turned up & I took a great fancy to her—a most capable and agreeable woman. . . . She hunted vigorously all day, motored to Paris after dinner & is today engaged in passing

Coco and her friends in the garden of her villa, La Pausa, 1938

and improving dresses on endless streams of mannequins. . . . Some have been altered ten times. She does it with her own fingers, pinning, cutting, looping, etc."

Another time, Coco and Churchill were guests at Bendor's Stack Lodge in Scotland. Churchill sent his wife a letter saying, "Coco is here . . . She fishes from morn till night & in two months has killed 50 salmon. She is [very] agreeable—really a [great] & strong being fit to rule a man or an Empire."

Coco opened a boutique in London's Mayfair district, near Bendor's town house. Socialites and aristocrats became her clients, and her English country look was a hit on both sides of the Atlantic.

Vogue announced: "Tweeds have made the practical beautiful and the beautiful practical."

Time magazine featured a story about Coco's growing success, describing "the light boyish sweaters which form the sports costume of many an American and English woman."

A story says Bendor paid tribute to Coco by having gold interlocking *C*s embossed on all the black lampposts in the city of Westminster. Later the Westminster City Council insisted that *CC* stood for "City Council." But it was also said that the duke's family quashed the legend of Bendor's homage to Coco.

Yet Bendor didn't propose marriage, as she hoped he would. Despite his love for her, he wanted a son to inherit his estate. By 1928, Coco was forty-five years old and could not have a child. Bendor became engaged to a young English noblewoman, and his romance with Coco ended. It was rumored that she was the one who rejected his proposal, saying, "There have been many Duchesses of Westminster, but only one Coco Chanel." In later years she denied having said anything so "vulgar." But she did say, "Salmon fishing is not a life. . . . I've always known when to leave."

Coco bought a tract of land on the French Riviera at Roquebrune-Cap-Martin as a Mediterranean retreat. She hired an architect to study the orphanage at Aubazine where she had grown up, because she wanted to duplicate its serenity and simplicity and the stone staircase at the entrance. Her palatial villa, La Pausa, was finished in 1929, and she hosted lavish weekend parties. Guests included artist Salvador Dalí, who painted a still life there, *L'Instant Sublime*, that depicted a snail, a telephone receiver, and a drop of water about to fall on a frying egg. Winston Churchill was also inspired to paint at the villa and did watercolors.

Another guest, Bettina Ballard, a reporter for *Vogue*, admired Coco's getup: "She wears navy jersey slacks with a slip-on sweater, and a bright red quilted bolero. Her red canvas espadrilles have thick cork soles—excellent for walking." In the evening Coco appeared in black velvet slacks and cashmere sweaters, outfits that are still popular today.

TAKE OFF
THE
GIRDLE!

○○○○○○○○○○○○○○○○○○○○○○○○○○○○○

By now Coco was one of the richest women in the world and employed 2,400 workers in twenty-six different studios. In 1929, at the peak of her fame, the Wall Street stock market crashed in the United States. The Great Depression that followed affected Europe as well as America. World trade collapsed. German, French, and then British industrial production decreased. In America, businesses went bust, and eventually nearly thirteen million people were unemployed.

Friends said that Coco panicked but hid her anxiety. She lost some wealthy clients who could no longer afford her clothes, which were the most expensive in Paris. However, there were still people rich enough to order haute couture workmanship. Coco reduced the prices of her evening dresses by replacing expensive fabrics such as lace and chiffon with cotton and organdy. And the greatest part of her own fortune came from Chanel Nº 5. The fragrance had become the world's bestselling perfume and provided a steady income.

I have said that black had everything. White too. They have an absolute beauty.

Ignoring the poverty found in France and elsewhere in the world, the "elegant" set in Paris continued to live the high life, including attending fancy-dress balls. In June 1930, socialites at the functions tried to outdo each other, and Coco designed many of their fantasy costumes. Some hosts asked guests to come disguised as someone that everyone knew by sight, and partygoers enjoyed cross-dressing. Journalist Janet Flanner wrote in *The New Yorker*, "Chanel did a land office business, cutting and fitting gowns for young men about town who appeared as some of the best-known women."

For another ball everyone was told to dress in white, and a number of women showed up in Coco's gowns. Coco loved white for its purity and simplicity. She liked white as a contrast to tanned skin, like hers, and often ended the unveiling of a new collection by presenting three white evening dresses. White and black were her signature colors, an influence from her days at Aubazine. "Women think of every color, except the absence of colors," she declared. "I have said that black had everything. White too. They have an absolute beauty."

At one event Coco met movie producer Samuel Goldwyn. She knew he was Jewish, but, putting aside her prejudice, she said, "There are great Jews." Goldwyn worried about dwindling ticket sales in America as the economic crisis worsened. He thought of luring middle-class audiences, especially women, to the movies by featuring the latest Paris fashions. So he invited Coco to come to Hollywood to design clothes for his stars on and off the stage. At first she refused, but when he promised to pay her a million dollars, she finally agreed and took Misia along as a traveling companion.

Back in 1927 Coco had designed a dress that actress Mary Pickford wore in a silent film called *My Best Girl*, about a young woman working in a five-and-dime store. Pickford's demure black dress made of crepe de chine had a white lace collar. The schoolgirl look—a black dress trimmed with white collar and cuffs—influenced by Coco's convent uniform, was one of her favorite styles. The color combination was ideally suited to movies, which were shot only in black-and-white at that time.

Mary Pickford wearing Chanel's little black dress
in a scene from the silent movie *My Best Girl*
costarring Buddy Rogers, 1927

Upon arriving in New York in 1931, Coco was mobbed
by reporters. In Hollywood she and Misia met the greatest
stars of the day: Greta Garbo, Marlene Dietrich, and Gloria
Swanson. Coco toured the studios and learned how films
were shot. Her assignment was to design clothes in Paris that
would be made by fitters in Hollywood and then completed
according to her instructions.

Back home at rue Cambon, Coco began making costumes
for Gloria Swanson's movie *Tonight or Never*, the story of an
opera singer. Swanson came to Paris for a fitting of her black

bias-cut satin gown. Coco thought Swanson was chubby and suggested that she lose a few pounds. When Swanson returned for a final fitting, she had gained weight. Coco "glared furiously at me," recalled Swanson. "I said I would try [the gown] with a girdle," but the line of the undergarment showed.

"Take off the girdle and lose five pounds," snapped Coco. The next day Swanson showed up with a roll of surgical elastic and begged Coco to have it made into "a rubberized undergarment" to make her look slim.

Coco refused. "Lose five pounds!" she commanded.

"Maybe I can't," said Swanson.

"Why not?"

"Reasons of health, maybe. Look, *just try it*."

Coco went along with the solution. "It took three people to get me into it," remembered Swanson, but it worked. Swanson looked stunning in the gown. It turned out that she had had a good reason for putting on weight: She was pregnant.

Swanson left with a whole wardrobe designed by Coco. But the movie was a flop, and it ended Coco's career in Hollywood. The movie moguls told her that "her dresses weren't sensational enough. She made a lady look like a lady." Many actresses stayed with her for their offscreen wardrobes, though, until a new competitor stole them away. Her name was Elsa Schiaparelli.

Schiaparelli's silk butterfly dress for evening, summer 1937

THAT
ITALIAN

○○○○○○○○○○○○○○○○○○○○○○○○○○○○○○

S chiap (pronounced *skap*), as she was called, came from a prosperous, intellectual, Italian family. In Paris she had risen to fame with her sporty separates (sweaters and skirts) and imaginative innovations. Schiap introduced a bold new color, shocking pink. She too was friends with Dalí and Cocteau and collaborated with them on zany surrealist designs: a gown printed with a life-size lobster, a hat shaped like an upside-down high-heeled pump. In 1935 Schiap opened her couture house on Place Vendôme, just down the street from the Ritz hotel. The Ritz was one of the most luxurious hotels in the world, with a superb dining room downstairs. Coco lived at the Ritz, and in the morning she left for work at her salon on rue Cambon, the street behind the hotel. So Schiap quipped, "Poor Chanel, I use the front door of the Ritz, she must use the back."

Coco detested Schiap and bitterly referred to her as "that Italian who's making clothes."

Schiap called Coco "that dreary little bourgeoise" (a middle-class woman).

Coco thought that Schiap would soon be finished, with her outrageous styles. Yet in 1934 *Time* claimed that Coco was no longer the leader in fashion. Instead they wrote, "Mme. Schiaparelli is the one to whom the word 'genius' is applied most often."

One evening the archrivals attended the same costume ball. The theme was an enchanted forest. Coco went dressed as herself, but Schiap disguised herself as a surrealist tree. "There was a near disaster," recalled Bettina Ballard, the Paris editor for *Vogue*, "when Chanel . . . dared Schiaparelli . . . to dance with her, and, with purposeful innocence, steered her into the candles." Schiap's costume caught fire. "The fire was put out—and so was Schiaparelli—by delighted guests squirting her with soda water," reported Ballard.

Schiap posed a serious threat to Coco throughout the '30s. She built her collections around themes such as music and the circus. Celebrities, socialites, and royalty vied for front-row seats at her exciting runway shows.

Coco's shows were "terribly sedate and a little bit dull," wrote Danish journalist Ragna Fischer. Coco stayed hidden at

Chanel's understated navy blue linen day suit with ribbed knit trim, 1937, in contrast to Schiaparelli's whimsical print dress

the top of her famous mirrored staircase as the models glided down. But she won rave reviews for her sleek, elegant dresses.

"The couture is swinging back to the great age of Chanel simplicity," announced *Vogue* in 1937. The magazine described her spring collection as "dignified elegance" and applauded her short-jacket suits as "un-sensational, subtle, wearable—[with] no tricks." Coco introduced silk linings for her suit jackets and sewed fine gilt chains into the bottoms of the jackets and the hemlines of the skirts to keep them weighted and in place. Her designs were timeless. One of her suits with ribbed knit trim at the collar, cuffs, and pockets would look stylish today.

Meanwhile, Schiap adopted the surrealist theme of metamorphosis for her spring collection that year and featured butterflies. Her designs appealed to women who wanted to have fun with fashion. Those who feared ridicule went with Chanel.

I DETEST
GIVING IN

○○○○○○○○○◯◯◯◯◯◯◯◯○○○○○○○○○

ut Coco had another worry aside from competition from Schiap. The political situation in France had changed drastically. In April 1936 a Jewish socialist, Léon Blum, was elected premier (prime minister). Coco and her elitist, anti-Semitic peers feared having a Jewish premier. Blum's left-wing government represented the working class and sought reforms such as paid vacations and unemployment insurance. Wealthy conservatives like Coco were terrified about how their businesses selling luxury goods would be affected by the promised changes. If they were forced to pay higher wages to their workers, they, the owners, would make less money. And if factories that produced fabrics stopped production during strikes, Coco would not have the materials necessary for making clothing.

Textile manufacturers *did* go on strike. Other strikers included railway workers, waiters in restaurants, bakers, and salespeople in department stores. The country was in turmoil. Demonstrators marched in the streets. Throughout France, thousands of workers went on strike to protect the new benefits enacted by Blum's government.

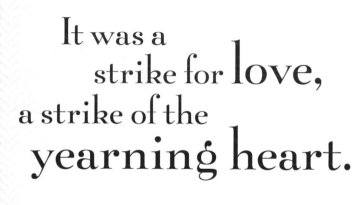

It was a strike for love, a strike of the yearning heart.

On June 2, 1936, Coco's entire staff at rue Cambon walked out. They demanded shorter hours and higher wages in the form of weekly salaries instead of payment for piecework. Coco's loyal private accountant, Madame Renard, slipped away to the Ritz and told her boss what had happened. She urged Coco to leave Paris for her own safety.

Coco wondered if her workers had gone crazy. "I decided to go and talk to the rebels," she said. Dressed in a navy blue suit and her *real* pearls, a visual contrast to her workers' condition,

she hurried over to rue Cambon. But the workers barred the entrance and wouldn't let her in. The sight of them enraged Coco. They argued. Coco refused to negotiate. "I detest giving in, bending over, humiliating myself," she told a friend.

From her point of view, her employees owed her nothing but gratitude. She maintained that she gave them "perfectly proper" wages. "My staff are always better paid than anyone else's," she said, "because I know what work is." She even provided vacations for certain employees. Every year she sent her "most delicate apprentices" to stay at a "workers' holiday

Chanel workers on strike, June 1936

camp" she had built in Mimizan in the Landes, a resort area on the Atlantic coast of France. Manon Ligeour, one of her top seamstresses, had gone there and appreciated the trip. Manon said, "The first time I saw the sea was at Mimizan."

Nevertheless, the three hundred strikers held fast. Most of them were not rewarded with trips to the seaside. They expected increased wages and paid vacations. Coco immediately fired all of them. But they stayed and organized a sit-in with music and dancing in the workrooms.

Later Coco reinvented the episode as "cheerful and delightful. The accordion could be heard playing all over the house," she recalled. According to her story, she asked the strikers what they wanted, and they replied, "We don't see enough of Mademoiselle. Only the models see her."

"It was a strike for love," she lied, "a strike of the yearning heart."

In reality, she denounced her employees and said, "Imagine women . . . staging a sit-down strike. . . . Very pretty. What idiots those girls were!"

Finally, Coco proposed selling her business to the workers, and they could pay themselves whatever they wished. She would remain as a consultant. Of course, the workers couldn't afford to buy her out, and after three more weeks on strike they settled with her. She agreed to some of their demands, although she really wanted to fire them all. But she couldn't shut down production any longer. Her lawyer and financial directors advised her to reach a solution by the end of June or she would be unable to present her fall collection. That would mean leaving the field wide open to her competitor, Elsa Schiaparelli, whose employees had never gone on strike because she had paid them well. The event left Coco's staff tense and resentful. They never forgot her indifference to their struggles despite their having helped make her one of the richest women in the world.

A Chanel gypsy-style dress that appeared in British *Vogue*, February 22, 1939

A
MISTAKE

○○○○○○○○◯◯◯◯◯◯◯◯◯◯○○○○○○○○

By 1938, war was threatening to erupt in Europe. Once again as Paris faced catastrophe, the mood was defiantly festive at all levels of society. Workers had jobs, tourists filled expensive hotels, and wealthy socialites partied. "We flitted from ball to ball," said a young designer, Christian Dior. "Fearing the inevitable cataclysm, we were determined to go down in a burst of splendor."

Coco, age fifty-five, caught the spirit and designed evening clothes that were more romantic. Coco chose the word "gypsy" to suggest a carefree, artistic quality. Gypsies, or Roma, had come from Bohemia. They lived in lower-class neighborhoods, as did struggling artists and musicians, who were therefore called bohemians. The gypsy style reimagined a picturesque look. Chanel's gypsy gowns reflected peasant dresses and had full gingham checked taffeta skirts and puff-sleeve embroidered blouses. Even her tailored day suits were decorated with colorful pom-poms and braids. Diana Vreeland, the future editor of *Harper's Bazaar*, wrote, "Everyone thinks of *suits* when they think of Chanel. . . . If you could have seen my clothes from Chanel in the thirties—the dégagé [free and easy] gypsy skirts, the divine brocades, the little boleros, the roses in the hair. . . . And the ribbons were so pretty."

We were determined to go down in a burst of splendor.

Vreeland had a gown from Coco's romantic period that she described as "the most beautiful dress I've ever owned." The skirt was made "of silver lamé, quilted in pearls . . . Then the bolero was lace entirely encrusted with pearls and diamanté; then, underneath the bolero was the most beautiful shirt of linen lace."

During the summer of 1938, Coco spent as much time as she could at her villa, La Pausa. Houseguests included her

An illustration of Chanel's "tricolor" evening dress with red, white, and blue floral embroidery, 1939

twelve-year-old grandniece and namesake, Gabrielle Palasse. Gabrielle was the daughter of Coco's nephew André. That summer, young Gabrielle remembered that they all "clustered around the radio, stupefied and petrified as they listened to the voice of Hitler."

In spring 1939, as war with Germany loomed, Coco introduced a patriotic collection featuring the French tricolor flag. She repeated the flag's bands of blue, white, and red in a charming organdy gown in one of her last collections before the outbreak of war.

This is not the time for making dresses.

"In those final, feverish weeks of freedom, the entire city seemed to be celebrating," recalled Diana Vreeland.

"Business is close to having a little boom," reported Janet Flanner, an American writer stationed in Paris. "It has taken the threat of war to make the French loosen up and have a really swell and civilized good time."

On September 1, 1939, Germany bombed Poland, and on September 3, France and Great Britain declared war on Germany. Three weeks later, Coco closed down the House of Chanel. Without notice, she laid off her entire staff. Only the boutique at 31, rue Cambon stayed open to sell costume jewelry and perfume.

"This is not the time for making dresses," she said, "nor for dressing the wives of husbands who are going to be killed."

However, people said that Coco shut down her business out of spite toward her workers, who had gone on strike in 1936. Others whispered that she felt overshadowed by Elsa Schiaparelli and used the war as an excuse to drop out of the competition. Later Coco claimed that she thought all the fashion houses in Paris would close. "I thought no one would go on making dresses," she said. "I was so stupid, such a *dummy* about life. . . . Well, I made a mistake. Some people sold dresses all through the war."

Schiap kept her business open, as did other leading fashion designers. They realized the importance of maintaining the dressmaking industry as a source of income for remaining workers and for the nation's morale. The French government approached Coco and begged her to reopen the House of Chanel for "the prestige of Paris." She refused. Then they asked her to show a little patriotic spirit by inventing new uniforms for women officers and nurses. "Me!" she exclaimed. "You must be joking!" No one could force her to do work she considered beneath her. "I had the feeling that we had reached the end of an era," said Coco, and she retired to her suite at the Ritz.

"The city had become, almost overnight, an empty city," wrote Carmel Snow, editor in chief of *Harper's Bazaar*. "You can walk for miles without seeing a child. Even the dogs—and you know how Parisians love their dogs—have been sent away."

In May 1940 Germany invaded France, and soldiers marched toward Paris. Coco packed some trunks and fled, as did Elsa Schiaparelli and millions of others. Coco and her maid drove to the Pyrenees to stay in the house that she had bought for her nephew André, who was now an officer in the army. Coco's grandniece Gabrielle remembered her Auntie Coco's grief when she heard of France's surrender to Germany on June 22. "We listened to the news on the radio, and she wept bitterly," recalled Gabrielle.

German troops marching into Paris with the Arc de Triomphe in the background, June 1940

HE ISN'T A GERMAN!

ooooooooOOOOOOOOooooooooo

Yet Coco grew restless during the summer and made her way back to Paris. The Nazis had occupied the city, but Hitler had decided not to destroy it. In August Coco returned to the Ritz and found that high-ranking German officers had taken over the hotel, including her grand suite. But the commandant allowed her to stay and gave her a small room. Coco carried on by avoiding the Nazis. She knew from surviving her difficult childhood how to make the best of a bad situation. German soldiers stood in line in front of the House of Chanel in the hope of being able to buy a bottle of perfume. "Idiots!" she sneered.

However, around this time she began dating a German intelligence officer, Baron Hans Günther von Dincklage, called Spatz (the Sparrow). Coco at age fifty-seven enjoyed the companionship of a charming younger man. She claimed she had met him before the war. Now Spatz visited her at her private apartment above the salon at rue Cambon. He wore civilian clothes, not a uniform, because he was a spy, a member of the Abwehr, the Nazi intelligence agency. He may even

Coco and Spatz in 1951 at Villars-sur-Ollon, Canton of Vaud, Switzerland

have been a double agent working for both the Nazis and the British. "He often came to see Mademoiselle at rue Cambon but we never saw him in uniform," wrote Coco's maid, Germaine Domenger, after the war in a letter defending Coco. Coco had been accused of collaborating with the Germans.

A friend warned Coco of the danger of having a relationship with a German, but Coco said of Spatz, "He isn't a German. His mother is English!" She and Spatz spoke English to each other. Coco later said they both loathed the war for disrupting their lives. Spatz had lived in Paris as a diplomat at the German embassy since 1928 and enjoyed dining in the best restaurants and yachting with his rich friends. During the war he and Coco didn't go out in public but had dinner parties at the homes of an inner circle that included others who had remained in Paris, among them Picasso, Cocteau, Colette, and Misia. Misia disapproved of Coco socializing with a German. She hated the occupation and the anti-Jewish laws. At one gathering, Misia dared to confront an important German official.

In 1941 Jews in occupied France were forbidden to engage in business and professional activities. The Wertheimers, who managed Coco's perfume and cosmetics business, were Jewish and had fled France in 1940. They made their way to New York City and continued producing Chanel N⁰ 5 in a factory in New Jersey. The Wertheimers sent a trusted American friend back to Paris to pick up the formula for the perfume from the company's office and to Grasse to buy the necessary ingredients and smuggle the materials into the United States.

Coco felt she now had the opportunity to seize full control of the company. Like many French citizens, she resented Jewish refugees living in France during the 1930s. When Léon Blum, who was a Jew, had become premier in 1936, his accession to power had triggered a hate campaign against Jews, even though he and his ancestors were French born.

Before the Wertheimers left France, they had asked their non-Jewish business associate Félix Amiot, an industrialist, to front for them as the new co-owner. Nazi storm troopers brought Amiot in for questioning and accused him of serving as a cover for the Wertheimers. Coco followed up with a letter to the administrator who decided what would happen to businesses left by anyone who had fled France. She insisted that her perfume business was "still the property of Jews" and had been "legally 'abandoned' by the owners. I have," she wrote, "an indisputable right of priority." However, the Wertheimers had transferred ownership to Amiot before leaving the country, and the arrangement was judged "legal and correct." So their partnership with Coco remained the same.

Sometimes Coco went to her villa on the Riviera. The architect who had designed La Pausa was a member of the local French Resistance group. Once, he asked her to intervene on behalf of a friend who had been arrested by the Gestapo, the German secret police, and she agreed. Unbeknownst to

Coco, the cellars of her villa were used to hide a transmitter and to provide a way station for Jews escaping from France to the Italian border. Today, we still don't know if she was a Nazi sympathizer or not. But what we do know is that what concerned her most was keeping and building her fortune after a childhood of poverty.

In the summer of 1943, Coco dreamed up a scheme to bring about peace talks. She spoke to Spatz's colleague Captain Theodor Momm and proposed that she act as a messenger to her old friend Winston Churchill, who was now the British prime minister. Captain Momm later testified that at first he hesitated but then decided to report her idea to the chief of Nazi intelligence in Berlin. Some of the senior commanders secretly wanted to negotiate with the Allies to end the war. Momm arranged for Coco to travel to Madrid, Spain, and meet with the British ambassador and Churchill. News had spread that Churchill would stop in Madrid on his way back from a conference in Tehran, Iran, with U.S. president Franklin D. Roosevelt and Soviet premier Joseph Stalin.

Coco's mission was code-named Operation Modellhut (Model Hat). She arrived in Madrid in December and checked into the Ritz hotel. At the British embassy, she learned that Churchill was ill. Word came that he had caught a "bad cold" after the conference in Tehran. But really he had pneumonia. From Tehran he had flown in secret to General Dwight D. Eisenhower's headquarters in Tunisia. Exhausted and in pain, Churchill suffered a heart attack and stayed in Tunisia to recover. Did he seriously consider meeting Coco? All we know is that the British ambassador in Madrid told her that Churchill could see no one because of his grave illness. So Coco's plan failed, and she returned home.

At last, on August 25, 1944, French and American troops liberated Paris. Coco had just turned sixty-one. In the streets people laughed and sang "La Marseillaise," the French national anthem. But those who had collaborated with the Germans were punished. Thousands were imprisoned. Malcolm Muggeridge, a British intelligence officer stationed in Paris, said, "Everyone was informing on everyone else." Women who had been the girlfriends of Germans had their heads shaved and were paraded through the streets past jeering mobs. Coco, of course, had been romantically involved with a German too.

Muggeridge marveled at her shrewd move to escape punishment. She put up a sign in the window of her boutique announcing that her perfume was free for American GIs. They immediately lined up for bottles of Chanel N⁰ 5 "and would have been outraged if the French police had touched a hair on her head." Booton Herndon, an interpreter in the Army Corps of Engineers, wrote, "There had been a shortage of [perfume] during the Occupation, of course, like anything else, but now suddenly it appeared. At the time the magic words in perfume were Chanel N⁰ 5." An American wartime nurse remembered that she couldn't bring home "an awful lot" of souvenirs. But there was one thing she treasured: "Chanel, the perfume."

Still, two men from the Forces Françaises de l'Intérieur arrested Coco and took her in for questioning. Before Coco left with them, she told her maid whom to contact if she didn't come back immediately. Coco was released three hours later, "after a telephone call from Churchill." She received an urgent message from someone unknown saying, "Don't lose a minute . . . get out of France." Within hours she took off in a chauffeured limousine for the safety of Switzerland.

Dior's New Look, the "Bar Suit," designed in 1947 and photographed in 1954

WHAT

A

HORROR!

ooooooooOOOOOOOOoooooooooo

After the war officially ended in 1945, Coco divided her time between Lausanne, Switzerland, and Paris and Roquebrune-Cap-Martin, France. For the next few years she led a quiet, leisurely life, taking long walks, shopping, and dining out. "She was deeply bored," recalled her grandniece Gabrielle, who visited her. Coco began to dictate stories about her life to a biographer, Pierre Galante. Galante interviewed Coco's friends and listened to anecdotes. Fashion didn't seem to interest Coco anymore, until one time when she was having lunch with a friend. The woman wore a blouse that Coco didn't like. Galante recorded that "Coco could not resist taking a pair of scissors and making a few changes on the spot."

Meanwhile, Elsa Schiaparelli had returned to Paris and was running her couture house again. Her faithful staff had kept the business alive during the war years. But Schiap had a hard time competing with younger designers, mostly men: Christian Dior, Jacques Fath, and Cristóbal Balenciaga. On

Just take a look at me.

February 12, 1947, Christian Dior presented his spring collection. The models swished out in feminine dresses featuring nipped-in waists and full skirts made of yards of fabric. Underneath the voluminous skirts they wore tight corsets, padding, and petticoats to achieve the silhouette. Carmel Snow, editor in chief of *Harper's Bazaar*, said to Dior, "Your dresses are wonderful, they have such a new look!" The name "New Look" stuck.

Coco read about Dior's triumph in the Swiss papers. She was furious. "Dressing women is not a man's job," she declared. "Fashion has become a joke, the designers have forgotten there are women inside the dresses. . . . Clothes must have a natural shape." Nevertheless, women loved the sensational outfits. Over the next few years Dior was acclaimed as the most famous designer in the world.

Coco's devoted friend Misia Sert came to see her in Switzerland. Misia was going blind and had become addicted to drugs. Shortly after a visit in September 1950, Misia went home to Paris, and her condition sharply declined. She became bedridden, and her maid sent for Coco, who arrived in time to sit with Misia as she died. The next morning Coco prepared Misia for the funeral. She did her makeup and hair, dressed her in white, and arranged her on a bank of white flowers—medieval French queens had worn white rather than black to express deepest mourning. Coco said of Misia, "She has been my only woman friend."

By 1953 Coco's partners in the perfume business, the Wertheimers, were designing new offices in New York City, where they had relocated and set up a company during the war. They asked Coco to come help them, so she traveled to the United States. Upon her arrival, reporters asked her what she thought of Dior and the New Look. Coco was wearing one of her own suits that she had designed before the war, and she answered, "Just take a look at me."

For three months she stayed with her friend Maggie van Zuylen. One day Coco saw Maggie "looking as though she'd been trussed into a green satin Dior evening gown, barely able to move." Coco was appalled. "All her life she had fought against the straitjacket of the corsetry that women had been forced to wear . . . and here were 'these gentlemen,' the new big names in fashion, turning the clock back."

When Maggie's daughter, Marie-Hélène, brought home a debutante gown for a ball, she tried it on for Coco. The boned and corseted bodice of the strapless dress cut across the young woman's front. "What a horror!" exclaimed Coco. Right then and there, she grabbed her trusty scissors and created a dress made from a huge red taffeta curtain. At the ball everyone asked Marie-Hélène who had designed her dazzling red gown. "That's what made [Coco] decide to go for a comeback," claimed Marie-Hélène years later.

I WILL
SHOW
THEM

∘∘∘∘∘∘∘∘○○○○◯◯◯○○○○∘∘∘∘∘∘∘∘

I n 1953, the Wertheimers agreed to finance Coco's plan to reopen her fashion house, because they believed it would boost sales of Chanel N⁰ 5. At age seventy, Coco sailed home to France and began assembling a team. She corresponded with Carmel Snow at *Harper's Bazaar* and wrote, "I thought it would be fun to work again. . . . You know I might one day create a new style adapted to today's living. . . . I feel that this time has come."

Rumors swept through Paris. "Mademoiselle Chanel is going to come back! Chanel is returning to couture!"

Coco told reporters, "I still have perhaps two or three things to say."

Coco pinning and fitting the shoulder of a coat directly
on a model backstage at the Chanel show, 1962

She hired fitters, cutters, pattern makers, and seamstresses. Coco asked some of her former employees to "come quickly." Manon Ligeour, who had started working for Coco at the age of thirteen and had headed her top workroom during the 1930s, would direct her new atelier. As a young apprentice, Manon had vacationed at Coco's villa at Mimizan. Now Coco completely trusted Manon, who made the clothes that Coco herself wore. For nearly a year Coco worked on the new collection.

Mademoiselle was a terror.

After a quick breakfast in her old suite at the Ritz, she would dash over to rue Cambon. Models in white smocks would be waiting. "One by one they were called before her, and with her face scrunched in a determined grimace, her scissors on a cord around her neck, a pile of pins nearby, once again she set to work."

Margot McIntyre, a Seattle-born model, remembered that "once *la pose* began—the period when the individual dresses are created and re-created—no one left the salon without a very good excuse. Mademoiselle was a terror, commanding, ridiculing, pinching and watching, standing up, sitting down, on her knees, on all fours."

"You're already tired?" Coco snapped at the models after several hours.

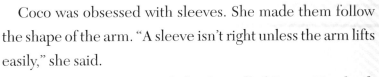

She was **always** snipping or taking out sleeves, driving the tailors absolutely **crazy.**

Coco was obsessed with sleeves. She made them follow the shape of the arm. "A sleeve isn't right unless the arm lifts easily," she said.

"Coco was a nut on armholes," recalled Diana Vreeland. "She never, ever got an armhole quite, *quite* perfect, the way she wanted it. She was always snipping and taking out sleeves, driving the tailors absolutely crazy." Every detail mattered.

The stripes on the sleeves of a plaid jacket, for example, had to perfectly match the stripes on the back. The silk linings of the jackets had overstitching to make the garments hold their shape. Coco had borrowed the idea from jackets worn by stable boys at the racetrack. And she added fine chains to the bottoms of the linings to make the jackets hang just right.

Coco seated on her mirrored staircase, watching the reactions of the audience as the models present her fashion show

Some jackets had false cuffs made of the same material as the sleeveless blouse underneath. A woman wearing the outfit would look finished yet not be too warm. Gilt buttons were embossed with one of Coco's favorite symbols: the double C, camellias, or a lion's head representing her star sign, Leo.

Skirts had to move easily, with the pockets falling at the right place for hands to slide into. Zippers were concealed in the stripes of a plaid. Chains weighted the hems of the skirts, too, so that they would hang perfectly, like the jackets. On the night before her show, Coco ripped apart seams and redid them to make sure "the underside is as perfect as the outside." She lay stomach down on the floor and had the models parade in front of her to check that every hem was stitched correctly.

Once you're faded, it takes more than a name and memories of past triumphs to put you back in the spotlight.

Coco continued to cut her models' hair as part of the ritual of offering a new collection. But one of her favorite models, Suzy Parker, objected. Although Suzy "worshiped at Chanel's feet," and "learned to stand like Chanel" and "wear her clothes with ease, [she] never went so far as to cut off her long, glamorous red hair, which Chanel deplored."

At last, on February 5, 1954 (once again to coincide with her lucky number), Coco presented her new collection. It included suits for daytime and evening as well as gowns made of black lace and gold brocade. As always, she crouched at the top of the mirrored staircase with a few friends as the models glided through the salon below. Coco was anxious. Fearful. Eager to be loved and accepted through her work as she had never been in her miserable childhood. When the show ended, there was a moment of icy silence. People left. Coco immediately dashed upstairs to her private apartment to avoid visitors. She was devastated. The French were not ready to forgive her for associating with a German during the war. In a note written by Elsa Schiaparelli's biographer, Palmer White, he recalled France's "antagonism" toward Chanel because of her "pro-Nazi activities."

European critics sneered that her clothes were dated.

"Chanel Dress Show a Fiasco!" read the headlines in London's *Daily Express*. "How sad are these attempts to make a comeback," wrote Marge Proops in the *Daily Herald*. "Once you're faded, it takes more than a name and memories of past triumphs to put you back in the spotlight."

French *Vogue* hated the collection.

Americans, however, loved it.

Life magazine ran a four-page spread about Coco's comeback. "At 71, she brings us more than a style—she has caused a veritable tempest. She has decided to return and to conquer her old position—the first."

In March, Bettina Ballard, the Paris editor of American *Vogue*, featured three pages of Chanel's clothes. Ballard opened the issue with a navy blue jersey schoolgirl/schoolboy suit and crisp white blouse from the comeback collection. "I wanted this costume for myself," she said. So she bought it and wore it to a meeting in New York, where retailers saw the latest Paris fashions. Bettina stood up in her Chanel suit and said, "Mark my words; this is the beginning of a new thing."

And it was. Orders poured in from the United States. Coco said, "I want to go on, go on and win."

When she presented her second return collection in the summer of 1954, French critics at last applauded her. "Paris Has Rediscovered Her Chanel!" declared one headline. "Chanel Is Once Again Chanel!" said another.

Dior's New Look faded away. Women were tired of cinched-in waists. They wanted something "graceful and easy" to wear that gave them confidence.

Chanel's "comeback suit," 1954, with a cardigan jacket and pocketed skirt

A fashion critic wrote, "Chanel has the secret of making those timeless clothes . . . which always look elegant."

When an interviewer asked Coco about the poor response she had first received, she said, "I thought, I will show them! In America there was great enthusiasm. In France I had to fight. But I did not mind. I love very much to battle. Now, in France they are trying to adapt my ideas. So much the better!"

Just as Dior had predicted that Paris would "go down in a burst of splendor," Coco had come back "in a burst of splendor."

EPILOGUE
A Very Bad Dead Person

During the 1950s, Coco worked on new collections. Never tiring, she kept her models standing in *"la pose"* for long hours as she draped and pinned cloth. She refined her classic suit, varying details and fabrics, and created iconic accessories.

On February 5, 1955, Coco introduced a quilted leather shoulder bag with a chain strap. She named the bag the 2.55 for the date of its launch. Next she presented sling-back pumps with contrasting toe caps.

Bettina Ballard wrote, "Now there is a whole new generation aware of the good-taste connotations of the 'Chanel Look.'" Coco's following included movie stars as well as celebrities such as Princess Grace of Monaco and Jacqueline Kennedy, wife of president John F. Kennedy.

In September 1957, Coco received an award from the Neiman Marcus department store for being the most influential designer of the twentieth century. The poor little peasant girl from an orphanage had conquered the world of fashion.

When asked why she had been in retirement for so long, Coco replied, "Never was I really in retirement in my heart. Always I observed the new clothes."

Chanel's 2.55 quilted leather handbag with a chain strap designed for comfort

Throughout the 1960s, when Coco was in her eighties, she competed with young designers. "[Yves] Saint Laurent has excellent taste," she said. "The more he copies me, the better taste he displays." Despite severe arthritis, she kept wielding her scissors.

Coco said, "I must think of my collection, because that's the future." On Sunday, January 10, 1971, she said to her assistant, "I'll be working tomorrow."

That evening Coco died. She was eighty-eight. Her maid dressed her in a white suit and blouse. Masses of white flowers covered her casket. She had requested to be buried in Lausanne, Switzerland, because she felt safe there. At the funeral, her models paid tribute to her with a floral sculpture in the shape of a giant pair of scissors that sat on top of the coffin.

Coco had once said, "I would make a very bad dead person, because once I was put under, I would grow restless and would think only of returning to earth and starting all over again."

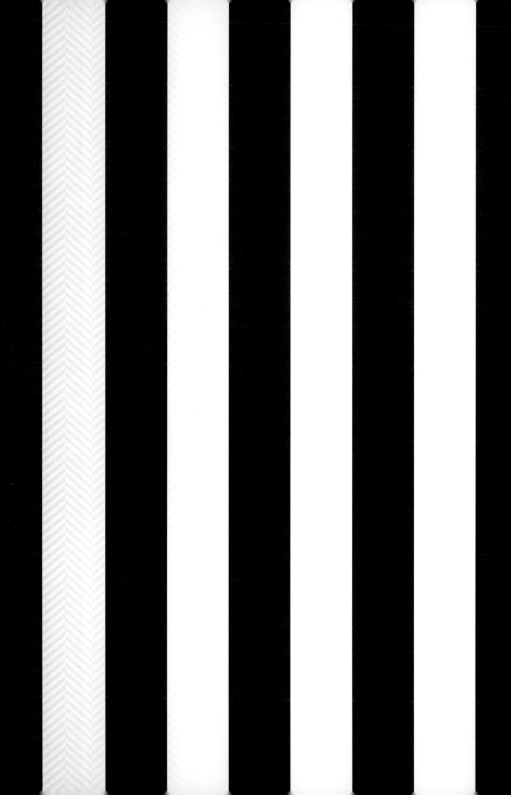

Where to See the Work of Coco Chanel

Museums throughout the world have collected and preserved Coco Chanel's designs, from hats and handbags to suits, shoes, and gowns. These are some of the places where her work can be seen.

North America

Kent State University Art Museum, Helen O. Borowitz
    Collection, Kent, Ohio

Los Angeles County Museum of Art, Costume and Textiles,
    Los Angeles

Metropolitan Museum of Art, Costume Institute,
    New York

Museum of the City of New York, New York

Museum of Fine Arts, Boston, Massachusetts

Philadelphia Museum of Art, Costume and Textiles
    Collection, Philadelphia, Pennsylvania

Phoenix Art Museum, Arizona Costume Institute, Phoenix,
  Arizona
Royal Ontario Museum, Toronto, Canada

Europe
Deutsche Kinemathek, Museum für Film und Fernsehen,
  Marlene Dietrich Collection, Berlin
Musée de la Mode de la Ville de Paris (Palais Galliera),
  Paris
Musée des Arts Décoratifs, Musée de la Mode et du
  Textile, Paris
Victoria and Albert Museum, Fashion Collection, London

Asia
Kyoto Costume Institute, Kyoto, Japan
Museum of Contemporary Art, Shanghai, China

Chanel's Fashion Firsts

This book is focused on Coco Chanel's contributions to the world of fashion and art. She introduced many "firsts" that are still popular today.

- The little black dress
- Chanel N⁰ 5 perfume
- Quilted handbag with chain strap
- Two-tone sling-back pumps
- Trousers for women
- Striped sailor's shirts for women
- Men's sweaters for women
- Men's ties for women
- Straw boater hats
- Short hair for women
- Large pockets on jackets for women
- Tweed collarless suits with braid-trimmed jackets
- Chains sewn into hems to make jackets and skirts hang perfectly
- Signature buttons
- Velvet hair bows
- Costume jewelry: fake pearls, as well as brooches, necklaces, and bracelets with glass stones
- Bright red lipstick in a push-up case
- Camellias made of fabric, leather, metal, and glass as accessories

Source Notes

Introduction

Page vii—"I make . . . comfortable in." Picardie, Justine.
Chanel: Her Life (Göttingen, Germany: Steidl, 2011),
p. 324.

Page vii—"Chanel is . . . greatest figure." Morand, Paul.
The Allure of Chanel, trans. Euan Cameron (London:
Pushkin Press, 2008), p. 181.

Page viii—"All her . . . into women's." Koda, Harold, and
Andrew Bolton. *Chanel* (New York: The Metropolitan
Museum of Art, 2005), p. 38.

Sell Her to the Gypsies

Page 1—"Chasnel." Madsen, Axel. *Coco Chanel:
A Biography* (London: Bloomsbury, 1990), p. 4.

Page 2—"Gabrielle." Madsen, p. 6.

Page 2—"Little Coco." Haedrich, Marcel. *Coco Chanel:
Her Life, Her Secrets*, trans. Charles Lam Markmann
(Boston: Little, Brown, 1972), p. 23.

Page 2—"No childhood . . . serious matter." Morand, p. 22.

Page 3—"For the first . . . the gypsies." Morand, p. 23.

Page 3—"I was . . . secret garden." Picardie, p. 21.

I Am Not an Orphan!

Page 5—"I Am Not an Orphan!" Haedrich, p. 125.

Page 5—"My aunts . . . their house." Picardie, p. 26.

Page 7—"Chanel's anti-Semitism . . . often embarrassing." Vaughan, Hal. *Sleeping With the Enemy: Coco Chanel's Secret War* (New York: Alfred A. Knopf, 2011), p. 4.

Page 7—"We cut . . . all together." Chaney, Lisa. *Coco Chanel: An Intimate Life* (New York: Viking, 2011), p. 22.

Page 7—"Those novels . . . my pride." Morand, p. 20.

Page 8—"It had . . . or sixteen." Madsen, p. 16.

Page 10—"Vichy was . . . of them." Morand, p. 28.

Who Has Seen Coco?

Page 12—"I've lost . . . seen Coco?" Madsen, p. 26.

Page 12—"*la petite* Coco." Madsen, p. 26.

Page 12—"You won't . . . a trombone." Charles-Roux, Edmonde. *Chanel: Her Life, Her World, the Woman Behind the Legend*, trans. Nancy Amphoux (London: MacLehose Press, 2009), p. 76.

Page 13—"How lucky . . . have racehorses!" Morand, p. 29.

Page 13—"too young . . . from home." Picardie, p. 46.

Page 13—"I had . . . miserable childhood." Picardie, p. 46.

Pages 13–14—"She was . . . on horseback." Chaney, p. 47.

Page 14—"Whoever makes your hats?" Charles-Roux, p. 117.

Page 14—"I can't . . . to work." Madsen, p. 47.

Page 15—"Forgive me . . . love him." Madsen, p. 50.

Page 15—"I lied . . . a bit." Madsen, p. 55.

Page 16—"He really . . . you imagine?" Haedrich, p. 86.

Page 16—"I just . . . at *you*." Madsen, p. 57.

Page 16—"The more . . . to sell." Morand, p. 37.

Page 16—"Coco is . . . a businesswoman." Madsen, p. 57.

Page 18—"Paul Poiret . . . in costumes." Morand, p. 51.

Page 18—"We ought . . . of shock." Picardie, p. 92.

I Was My Own Master

Page 19—"best man." Madsen, p. 54.

Page 21—"Gabrielle Chanel." Garelick, Rhonda K. *Mademoiselle: Coco Chanel and the Pulse of History* (New York: Random House, 2014), p. 68.

Page 21—"trendy new boutique." Garelick, p. 68.

Page 21—"Where did . . . in Deauville." Madsen, p. 69.

Page 21—"Everybody wanted . . . as stars." Madsen, pp. 69–70.

Page 23—"The jersey . . . on top." Morand, p. 46.

Page 23—"I created . . . new silhouette." Garelick, p. 86.

Page 23—"Mademoiselle was . . . exceedingly simple." Madsen, p. 80.

Page 23—"Chanel's charming chemise dress." Madsen, p. 80.

Page 25—"By inventing . . . the waist." Morand, p. 45.

Page 25—"slim like Coco." Morand, p. 46.

Page 25—"Our workrooms . . . veritable rainbow."
Chaney, p. 113.

Page 27—"I took . . . braid off." Picardie, p. 105.

Page 27—"a young . . . little shepherd." Morand, p. 46.

Page 27—"In 1917 . . . into raptures." Morand, p. 46.

Page 27—"I was . . . myself alone." Picardie, p. 96.

Page 29—"His death . . . to me." Morand, p. 54.

Page 29—"1919 . . . lost everything." Garelick, p. 104.

Black Wipes Out Everything

Page 33—"Obviously I . . . completely bewitching."
Picardie, p. 116.

Page 33—"I tried . . . distract her." Vaughan, p. 13.

Page 33—"Because she . . . our age." Picardie, p. 124.

Pages 33–34—"All those . . . in black." Morand, p. 47.

Page 34—"the little black dress." Picardie, p. 129;
Madsen, p. 117.

Page 34—"I imposed . . . else around." Morand, p. 47.

Page 34—"little black dress." Bott, Danièle. *Chanel:
Collections and Creations* (London: Thames & Hudson,
2007), p. 164.

Page 35—"Ford dress." Bott, p. 168.

Page 35—"You have . . . achieved this." Garelick, p. 151.

Lead Them by the Nose

Page 37—"Women wear . . . you like." Picardie, p. 135.

Page 37—"I don't . . . is composed." Madsen, p. 133.

Page 38—"with a passion." Chaney, p. 187.

Page 38—"That's what . . . ever made." Madsen, p. 134.

Page 40—"Now I . . . sell this." Picardie, p. 136.

Page 40—"You've got . . . the nose." Picardie, p. 136.

Page 40—"You mean . . . *my* perfume?" Madsen, p. 135.

Page 40—"gold liquid within." Fiemeyer, Isabelle.
Intimate Chanel (Paris: Flammarion, 2011), p. 82.

Page 40—"We experimented . . . lottery ticket."
Madsen, p. 135.

Page 42—"I let . . . be swindled." Chaney, p. 228.

Page 42—"that bandit . . . bloody woman." Madsen, p. 137.

Go and Fetch My Pearls

Page 44—"naked." de la Haye, Amy, and Shelley Tobin.
Chanel: The Couturiere at Work (Woodstock, NY:
Overlook Press, 1994), p. 101.

Page 44—"Go and . . . my neck." Bott, p. 109.

Page 44—"I couldn't . . . false ones." Madsen, p. 153.

Page 44—"Expensive jewelry . . . remain so."
Morand, p. 122.

Page 46—"Slav period." de la Haye and Tobin, p. 31.

Page 46—"This unusual . . . right time." Marie, Grand
Duchess of Russia. *A Princess in Exile* (New York:
Viking Press, 1932), p. 160.

Page 47—"I watched . . . the pins." Marie, pp. 172–73.

Page 47—"Stand straight, girl." Madsen, p. 161.

Pages 47–49—"No one . . . of anybody." Marie, p. 173.

Page 49—"began to . . . out loud." Marie, p. 177.

Page 50—"The Peasant Look." de la Haye and Tobin, p. 32.

Page 50—"It is . . . look prosperous." Marie, p. 190.

Page 50—"a giant . . . her head." Garelick, p. 150.

Page 50—"When she . . . degree presentable." Marie, p. 190.

Pages 51–53—"Come to . . . you can." Madsen, p. 295.

Page 53—"It's disgusting . . . be rich." Wallach,
   Janet. *Chanel: Her Style and Her Life* (New York:
   Doubleday, 1998), p. 87.

Pages 54–55—"The famous . . . looping, etc." Chaney, p.
   244.

Page 55—"Coco is . . . an Empire." Chaney, p. 244.

Page 55—"Tweeds have . . . beautiful practical." Garelick,
   p. 196.

Page 55—"the light . . . English woman." Garelick, p. 196.

Page 56—"There have . . . Coco Chanel." Picardie, p. 202.

Page 56—"vulgar." Fiemeyer, p. 143.

Page 56—"Salmon fishing . . . to leave." Garelick, p. 216.

Page 56—"She wears . . . for walking." Picardie, p. 211.

Take Off the Girdle!

Page 58—"elegant." Haedrich, p. 65.

Page 58—"Chanel did . . . best-known women."
   Wallach, pp. 91–92.

Page 59—"Women think . . . absolute beauty."
 Picardie, p. 217.
Page 59—"There are great Jews." Vaughan, p. 70.
Page 61—"glared furiously . . . a girdle." Picardie, p. 231.
Page 61—"Take off . . . rubberized undergarment."
 Picardie, p. 231.
Page 61—"Lose five . . . *try it*." Madsen, p. 193.
Page 61—"It took . . . into it." Picardie, p. 231.
Page 61—"her dresses . . . a lady." Picardie, p. 232.

That Italian

Page 64—"Poor Chanel . . . the back." Madsen, p. 200.
Page 64—"that Italian . . . making clothes." White,
 Palmer. *Elsa Schiaparelli: Empress of Paris Fashion*
 (London: Aurum Press, 1996), p. 92.
Page 64—"that dreary little bourgeoise." White, p. 92.
Page 64—"Mme. Schiaparelli . . . most often."
 Chaney, p. 277.
Page 64—"There was a . . . soda water." Ballard, Bettina.
 In My Fashion (New York: D. McKay, 1960), p. 140.
Page 64—"terribly sedate . . . bit dull." Madsen, p. 218.
Page 66—"The couture . . . no tricks." Garelick, p. 253.

I Detest Giving In

Page 68—"I decided . . . the rebels." Morand, p. 123.
Page 69—"I detest . . . humiliating myself." Garelick, p. 257.

Page 69—"perfectly proper." Charles-Roux, p. 323.

Page 69—"My staff . . . work is." Morand, p. 125.

Pages 69–72—"most delicate . . . holiday camp."
Charles-Roux, p. 323.

Page 72—"The first . . . at Mimizan." Vaughan, p. 105.

Page 72—"cheerful and . . . yearning heart." Morand, p. 125.

Page 72—"Imagine women . . . girls were!" Garelick, p. 258.

A Mistake

Page 75—"We flitted . . . of splendor." Picardie, p. 290.

Page 76—"Everyone thinks . . . so pretty." Madsen, p. 219.

Page 76—"the most . . . linen lace." Stuart, Amanda
Mackenzie. *Empress of Fashion: A Life of Diana
Vreeland* (New York: HarperCollins, 2012), p. 85.

Page 78—"clustered around . . . of Hitler." Fiemeyer, p. 169.

Page 78—"In those . . . good time." Picardie, p. 291.

Page 79—"This is . . . be killed." Fiemeyer, p. 169.

Page 79—"I thought . . . the war." Haedrich, pp. 141–142.

Page 79—"the prestige of Paris." Chaney, p. 288.

Page 79—"Me! . . . You . . . be joking!" Charles-Roux, p. 331.

Page 79—"I had . . . an era." Garelick, p. 305.

Page 80—"The city . . . sent away." Picardie, p. 292.

Page 80—"We listened . . . wept bitterly." Picardie, p. 294.

He Isn't a German!

Page 81—"Idiots!" Haedrich, p. 152.

Page 83—"He often . . . in uniform." Picardie, p. 296.

Page 83—"He isn't . . . is English!" Haedrich, p. 152.

Page 84—"Still the . . . of priority." Mazzeo, Tilar J. *The Secret of Chanel Nº 5: The Intimate History of the World's Most Famous Perfume* (New York: HarperCollins, 2010), p. 152.

Page 84—"legal and correct." Mazzeo, p. 154.

Page 85—"bad cold." Madsen, p. 256.

Page 86—"Everyone was . . . everyone else." Picardie, p. 307.

Page 86—"and would . . . her head." Vaughan, p. 211.

Page 86—"There had . . . Chanel Nº 5." Herndon, Booton. "Paris Was Yesterday." *Virginia Quarterly Review* 70, no. 4 (1994), www.vqronline.org/essay/paris-was-yesterday.

Pages 86–87—"an awful . . . the perfume." Mazzeo, p. 149.

Page 87—"after a . . . from Churchill." Fiemeyer, p. 177.

Page 87—"Don't lose . . . of France." Vaughan, p. 210.

What a Horror!

Page 89—"She was . . . bored." Fiemeyer, p. 180.

Page 89—"Coco could . . . the spot." Vaughan, p. 235.

Page 90—"Your dresses . . . new look!" Chaney, p. 352.

Page 90—"Dressing women . . . man's job." de la Haye and Tobin, p. 88.

Pages 90–91—"Fashion has . . . natural shape." Garelick, p. 370.

Page 91—"She has . . . woman friend." Morand, p. 65.

Page 91—"Just take . . . at me." Chaney, p. 354.

Pages 91–92—"looking as . . . clock back." Fiemeyer, p. 184.

Page 92—"What a . . . a comeback." Madsen, p. 281.

I Will Show Them

Page 93—"I thought . . . has come." Vaughan, p. 237.

Page 93—"Mademoiselle Chanel . . . to say."
Vaughan, p. 237.

Page 96—"come quickly." Garelick, p. 372.

Page 96—"One by . . . to work." Wallach, p. 144.

Pages 96–97—"Once *la pose* . . . all fours." Madsen, p. 306.

Page 97—"You're already tired?" Madsen, p. 306.

Page 97—"A sleeve . . . lifts easily." Shaeffer, Claire B.
*Couture Sewing: The Couture Cardigan Jacket: Sewing
Secrets from a Chanel Collector* (Newtown, CT:
Taunton Press, 2013), p. 87.

Page 97—"Coco was . . . absolutely crazy." de la Haye and
Tobin, p. 31; Stuart, p. 86.

Page 100—"the underside . . . the outside." Wallach, p. 144.

Page 101—"worshiped at . . . Chanel deplored."
Picardie, p. 377.

Page 101—"antagonism . . . pro-Nazi activities."
Garelick, p. 378.

Page 101—"Chanel Dress . . . a Fiasco!" Chaney, p. 363.

Pages 101–102—"How sad . . . the spotlight." de la Haye and Tobin, p. 90.

Page 102—"At 71 . . . the first." Garelick, p. 378.

Page 102—"I wanted . . . for myself." Picardie, p. 326.

Page 102—"Mark my . . . new thing." Chaney, p. 365.

Page 102—"I want . . . and win." Madsen, p. 289.

Page 102—"Paris Has . . . Again Chanel!" Garelick, pp. 382–83.

Page 102—"graceful and easy." Garelick, p. 379.

Page 104—"Chanel has . . . look elegant." Garelick, p. 383.

Page 104—"I thought . . . the better!" Chaney, p. 368.

Page 104—"go down . . . of splendor." Picardie, p. 290.

A Very Bad Dead Person

Page 105—"*la pose.*" Madsen, p. 306

Page 105—"Now there . . . Chanel Look." Chaney, p. 371.

Page 105—"Never was . . . new clothes." Picardie, p. 337.

Page 106—"[Yves] Saint . . . he displays." Madsen, p. 298.

Page 106—"I must . . . working tomorrow." Chaney, pp. 389–90.

Page 107—"I would . . . over again." Morand, p. 175.

Bibliography

Books

Ballard, Bettina. *In My Fashion*. New York: D. McKay, 1960.

Bott, Danièle. *Chanel: Collections and Creations*. London: Thames & Hudson, 2007.

Caron, Vicki. *The Path to Vichy: Antisemitism in France in the 1930s*. Washington, D.C.: United States Holocaust Memorial Museum, Center for Advanced Holocaust Studies, 2005. www.ushmm.org/m/pdfs/Publication_OP_2005-07-02.pdf.

Chaney, Lisa. *Coco Chanel: An Intimate Life*. New York: Viking, 2011.

Charles-Roux, Edmonde. *Chanel: Her Life, Her World, the Woman Behind the Legend*. Translated by Nancy Amphoux. London: MacLehose Press, 2009.

de la Haye, Amy. *Chanel: Couture and Industry*. London: V&A Publishing, 2011.

de la Haye, Amy, and Shelley Tobin. *Chanel, the Couturiere at Work*. Woodstock, NY: Overlook Press, 1994.

Fiemeyer, Isabelle. *Intimate Chanel*. Paris: Flammarion, 2011.

Flanner, Janet. *Paris Was Yesterday, 1925–1939*. Edited by Irving Drutman. New York: Viking Press, 1972.

Garelick, Rhonda K. *Mademoiselle: Coco Chanel and the Pulse of History*. New York: Random House, 2014.

Gilbert, Martin. *Churchill: A Life*. New York: Holt, 1992.

Haedrich, Marcel. *Coco Chanel: Her Life, Her Secrets*. Translated by Charles Lam Markmann. Boston: Little, Brown, 1972.

Madsen, Axel. *Coco Chanel: A Biography*. London: Bloomsbury, 1990.

Marie, Grand Duchess of Russia. *A Princess in Exile*. New York: Viking Press, 1932.

Matthews, Elizabeth. *Different Like Coco*. Cambridge, MA: Candlewick Press, 2007.

Mazzeo, Tilar J. *The Secret of Chanel Nº 5: The Intimate History of the World's Most Famous Perfume*. New York: HarperCollins, 2010.

Morand, Paul. *The Allure of Chanel*. Translated by Euan Cameron. London: Pushkin Press, 2008.

Picardie, Justine. *Chanel: Her Life*. Göttingen, Germany: Steidl, 2011.

Rubin, Susan Goldman. *Hot Pink: The Life and Fashions of Elsa Schiaparelli*. New York: Abrams Books for Young Readers, 2015.

Shaeffer, Claire B. *Couture Sewing: The Couture Cardigan Jacket: Sewing Secrets from a Chanel Collector*. Newtown, CT: The Taunton Press, 2013.

Stuart, Amanda Mackenzie. *Empress of Fashion: A Life of Diana Vreeland*. New York: HarperCollins, 2012.

van Haeringen, Annemarie. *Coco and the Little Black Dress*. New York: NorthSouth Books, 2015.

Vaughan, Hal. *Sleeping with the Enemy: Coco Chanel's Secret War*. New York: Alfred A. Knopf, 2011.

Wallach, Janet. *Chanel: Her Style and Her Life*. New York: Doubleday, 1998.

White, Palmer. *Elsa Schiaparelli: Empress of Paris Fashion*. London: Aurum Press, 1996.

Catalogs

Koda, Harold, and Andrew Bolton. *Chanel*. New York: The Metropolitan Museum of Art, 2005.

Articles

Flanner, Janet. "31, rue Cambon." *The New Yorker*, March 14, 1931; www.newyorker.com/magazine/1931/03/14.

Herndon, Booton. "Paris Was Yesterday." *Virginia Quarterly Review* 70, no. 4 (1994); www.vqronline.org/essay/paris-was-yesterday.

"In True Form: Claire Shaeffer Demystifies Couture." *Palm Springs Life*, November 2008; www.palmspringslife.com/in-true-form.

Interviews

Clarissa M. Esguerra (assistant curator, Costume and Textiles, Los Angeles County Museum of Art), in discussion with the author, Los Angeles, February 11, 2016.

Claire B. Shaeffer (sewing expert, teacher, and Chanel scholar), in discussion with the author, Palm Springs, CA, February 22, 2016.

Acknowledgements: When my editor, Howard Reeves, asked me if I would be interested in doing a book on Coco Chanel, I immediately said YES! So I thank Howard for giving me a chance to study the life and work of this fascinating woman. At Abrams, I also appreciate the help of Masha Gunic, editorial assistant; Erich Lazar, the brilliant book designer who enhanced the beauty of every page; Pam Notarantonio, associate art director; and Amy Vreeland, managing editor. And my thanks to Warren Drabek of Express Permissions for tracking down images.

Many people helped me research and understand Chanel's work. I'm particularly grateful to Clarissa M. Esguerra, Nancy Carcione, and Leigh Wishner at the Costume and Textiles Department of the Los Angeles County Museum of Art for giving me a private viewing of Chanel's vintage clothing. An extra thank you to Nancy for finding vital information in the department's library. I also want to thank Claire Shaeffer, a scholar on Chanel couture construction techniques, for showing me vintage pieces from her own collection and explaining the exquisite tailoring.

A huge thank you to my agent, Kevin O'Connor, for his advice and support. And I thank my husband Michael Rubin for hunting down Coco's logo on lampposts in Westminster, London, and taking pictures. As always, I'm indebted to my son, Andrew, for his invaluable technical assistance. Enormous thanks to my friends at Lunch Bunch for their critiques and interest, and a special shout-out to Martha Tolles for lending me her Chanel suit and blouse and giving me the pleasure of wearing the real thing.

Index